T0348310

EVERY BABY NAME
(RUINED)

Brian Kerr

Every Baby Name (Ruined)

Congratulations!

You are going to have a baby. Or, you have a child between 0 and 16 without a name, in which case there are other areas of your life that will need attention after you have read this book.

Either way, you are about to choose a small word that will have a big impact. Your child's name will be with them forever — friends, partners, prime ministers and presidents will come and go, but their name will persist. It will determine their place in their school class register, their place on their work email list and their place on the nursing home's bedpan-emptying rotation. It's what they will write on their first cherished book, their wedding certificate and, if you call them Jayden, on their eventual release papers.

Yes, nominative determinism — the idea that our names influence what we end up doing with our lives — is real. Thomas Crapper invented the toilet. Usain Bolt is a very fast runner. And John Carpenter directs movies, whose sets are made out of wood. But beyond the literal meaning of every name are the equally important cultural, historical and linguistic markers that go with them. These are particularly significant when it comes to the names given to us by our parents.

Perhaps *Wayne,* or *Amelia*, or *Percy* has been in your family for generations and you want to pass it on one more time. A family name can show strong connections to the past and a pride in one's lineage. Maybe these qualities will then be reflected in your offspring.

You could be a music fan and have *Bjork* or *Elvis* on the shortlist. Your child will have an immediate connection with fans of these artists, and may even be considered creative before they pick up a pen — or a plectrum.

Or, maybe you are an elven singer or a battery billionaire and, for some reason, X Æ A-Xii makes the most sense for your child.

However you come to it, the name you choose will impact how your child relates to the world, and how the world relates to them. That's what makes this book the most important one you will buy this week.

Choose wisely, and good luck. Don't fuck this up.

A

BOYS

Aaron

Can be shortened to *Ron*.
Are you OK with that?

Abraham

Biblical, in the sense that
it is biblically shit.

Adair

A name which also describes
what obliged you to choose it.

Adam

Responsible for the downfall
of mankind. See *Eden*, *Eve*.

Adolf

From the German meaning
'Read a fucking book,
I'm begging you.'

Adrian

Sounds too much like
'a drain', which, of course,
he will be (on your finances,
emotions, time, soul, etc.)

Aiden

The one with the -den suffix
who mostly does white collar
crimes. See *Jayden*, *Kayden*,
Brayden etc.

Alan

An anagram of anal.
Enough said.

Albert

Albert DeSalvo was better
known as the Boston Strangler.
Fortunately, he was stabbed
to death in prison, leaving
behind his name and, probably,
quite a lot of mess.

Alby

Alby advising you against this.

Alexander

Alexander the Great once got so drunk he burnt down a city. Most people get drunk and burn their toast. More like *Alexander* the Bellend.

Allen

Derived from the Greek word meaning 'little bit of metal you get to help assemble your Ikea furniture'.

Amani

Armani but from a guy in the pub.

Amos

From the Hebrew meaning 'burden'. Hey, at least you're being honest with him from the start, because children are a massive financial and emotional *Amos*.

Andrew

Aggressively bland.

Anis

Technically, you're completely fine with this one. And everybody else will definitely see it the same way.

Armani

A 'luxury' name, the main luxury being that your child has the luxury of telling people he's called something else.

Arnold

There is only one person in the world who can pull off the name *Arnold* and it's not your kid. *Hasta la vista*, baby name.

Art

Something people pretend to like.

Aston

See *Martin*.

Atlas

He won't be able to carry the world on his shoulders but he'll be able to tell you what the capital of Monglolia is (Ulaan Bataar).

Atticus

Where your dad used to store the spare bedus and the Christmas decorationsus. And all the old pornographyus.

Axel

Greasy car part.

B

BOYS

Baker

Blame yourself when he wakes up at 3am every day.

Barnaby

Anagram of 'Nar, baby'.

Baron

In the old days a *Baron* was somebody that owned a castle and was hated by everyone. Nowadays they don't have a castle.

Barron

See *Baron*.

Basil

See *Herb*.

Bear

Stinks of salmon and dead hikers.

Beau

Eau neau.

Beaux

Eaux neaux.

Bellamy

This is the sort of name that an adopted zoo animal would have. A nice little postcard every year from *Bellamy* the marmoset saying thank you for the $30, that he loves eating grapes and sleeping on his branch, and actually could you make it $40 next time?

Ben

See *Benjamin*.

Benjamin

Might end up a *Ben*, but might end up a *Benji*. Want to find out?

Benji

See *Benjamin*.

Bill

Something to avoid until it is absolutely necessary.

Billy

Adj. Possessing the qualities of something to avoid until it is absolutely necessary.

Bobby

British slang for a police officer. For reference, British slang for police officers includes *fuzz*, *filth* and *tit-heads*. So, it's in great company.

Bodie

This isn't a real name, it's a French person saying 'body'.

Bowie

David Bowie's name wasn't even David Bowie. It was David Jones. You've just done what he did and named your son after a big knife.

Braylen

Try saying it into a phone in front of three-inch glass.

Brent

The surname of Ricky Gervais'
intolerable boss character.
Forever associated with a
grating, boorish, attention
addict. And his intolerable
boss character.

Brian

Ancient Anglo-Saxon word
meaning 'photocopier salesman'.
Born with Coke-bottle glasses
and a novelty tie.

Brock

From the Old English meaning
'badger', an animal so
diseased that Britain has
ordered three culls in the
last ten years.

Bryan

Brian with his glasses off.
Still has the tie.

Bryn

Welsh word meaning 'hill'.
Something that tires you out
and is best avoided.

Bud

American for 'mate'. So it's
like you're calling him 'mate'
the whole time.

Buzz

More of a noise than a name.

Byron

The name *Byron* was
popularised by the famous
poet Lord *Byron* — a dirty
bastard prone to incest and
riddled with sexual diseases.

C

BOYS

Calvin

Printed on underwear the world over and therefore the name that is, on average, closest to piss and skidmarks at any given moment.

Cameron

A wannabe farmer, which is ridiculous because not even farmers want to be farmers. Wears those R.M. Williams boots but has never delivered a calf.

Carl

What a crow would call its son.

Carter

Carter is a second name. This is basic stuff.

Cash

Another darkly ironic name for a baby. You might as well name them *Sleep*, or *Social Life*.

Casper

The friendly ghost! (Of a dead child.)

Caspian

A stagnant body of water somewhere in Europe.

Cayden

See *Brayden*, *Jayden*, *Rayden* etc.

Cedric

From the Welsh for 'bounty', the chocolate bar nobody likes.

Charles

Charles Manson is synonymous with murder, but he was never actually convicted of killing anyone. What he did was, he got a lot of impressionable teenagers to do the murdering for him. It probably wouldn't work these days because there's shit like TikTok and vaping to keep them amused.

Clark

The opposite of Superman.

Claude

Sounds like a French cartoon cat with a beret and a distasteful attitude towards women.

Clay

A lumpen mass that needs to be physically beaten and put in an oven before it becomes anything useful. See *Klay*.

Clint

What a robot would say his name was if he was pretending to be human.

Clive

Clive comes from the Old English meaning for 'someone who lives near a cliff'. You'd have to be pretty proud of living near a cliff to name your son after it. It would have to be a very big part of your identity, wouldn't it? There are plenty of nice places to live that are near a cliff, but it's hard to imagine any are exceptional enough to saddle your son with the memory of.

Clyde

Clive with a cold.

Colin

From the Old Germanic word for 'man who loses virginity with a prostitute at the age of 45'.

Colt

Noun. Baby horse. Fine when he's 9, but taking the piss when he's 90.

Craig

There were three years in the 1980s when naming a baby *Craig* was acceptable. The *Craig* amnesty resulted in a *Craig* plague that devastated suburban Australia. Today there are suburbs in Perth and Adelaide where every man in his 30s is named *Craig*.

Curtis

A name even 50 Cent couldn't save.

Cyril

Cock-nosed antagonist from the Raccoons cartoon.

D

BOYS

Dale

See *Glen*.

Daley

How often you will regret choosing this name.

Dalton

AI-generated fake name for when writers need something to call a minor character.

Daly

See *Daley*.

Dane

Do you think Danish people name their sons *Australian?* They might, but it would be pretty weird.

Daniel

From the Latin meaning 'Only God can judge me', like those tattoos you see on people the police are looking for.

Darwin

Bearded nerd who pissed everybody off for a very long time.

David

Cartoonishly plain, if such a thing is possible. Like naming your dog Rover.

Dean

It is ironic that the most important person at a university is the 'dean', yet nobody named *Dean* has ever been to university.

Dennis

Born aged 47 with a sunburn and a taste for solo South Asian holidays.

Derick

See *Derrick*.

Derrick

One of those nodding contraptions that pumps oil out of the ground, which are named after gallows, which are named after Thomas *Derrick*, an executioner.

Dexter

Dexter was the name of a fictional serial killer who only killed the bad guys, thus posing some interesting questions around morality and justice. *Dexter* was also the name of the show itself, which went on for three seasons too long, thus posing some interesting questions around flogging a dead horse.

Diesel

Stinks, costs a lot of money, kills seabirds.

Dillon

Can be shortened to *Dill*, which is both a herb and Australian slang for a shitwit.

Doak

Another one of those noises that come out when Batman gets clobbered. See *Josh*.

Dominic

Will eventually bring a gun to chess club.

Donald

Plump, angry, mostly trouserless cartoon duck. Plump, angry, mostly trouserless former US president.

Drake

Noun. Male duck.
Prop. noun. Shitty rapper.

Drew

Andrew after getting blonde tips and one of those shark tooth necklaces.

Duke

See also *Baron, Earl*.

Dustin

Verb. Household chore.

Dwayne

Comes out holding a spanner in one hand and a spanner in the other.

Dylan

Overrated singer we don't have to pretend is good any more.

E

BOYS

Earl

See *Duke*, *Baron*.

Ebenezer

Fictional tightwad.

Eden

The place where *Adam* fucked up. See also *Eve*.

Edward

We're leaving *Edward* in 1895.

Elgin

A name so bad the musician Ginuwine decided to rename himself 'Ginuwine'.

Elliott

Anagram of 'toilet' … Almost. You checked, though, didn't you?

Elmer

Elmer is a name made popular by a glue and a pig.

Elon

Ancient Hebrew name meaning 'tree'. Modern South African name meaning 'man who sells exploding cars'.

Elvin

Sounds like some Dungeons and Dragons shit to me.

Elvis

From the Phoenician meaning
'portly, drug-addled
cock-thruster'.

Eric

See *Erica*.

Erik

See *Erika*.

Ernest

Adj. Serious. Because
everybody wants a solemn
child.

Esau

Statistically the first four
letters you pull out of
a Scrabble bag. Only four
points, too.

Ethan

Ancient Hebrew name meaning
'strong'. But babies aren't
strong? So what the fuck?

Evan

Evan worse than *Ethan*.

Everest

Covered in human shit and
responsible for over 300
deaths.

Ewan

Pronounced 'you-an'. As in
'you-an dad are bastards for
calling me Ewan'.

F

BOYS

Felix

The 'x' is doing a lot of heavy lifting in this Fauntelroy-esque first name.

Fergus

See *Cameron*.

Finn

Fish wing.

Fisher

Gender-neutral version of 'fisherman'.

Forest

A place where teenagers go to fuck and take drugs.

Forrest

See *Forest*.

Fox

Ginger vermin.

Francis

Something belonging to France.

Fraser

See *Carter*.

Freddie

They're all called shit like *Freddie* now. Choose something else.

Fritz

A word used when something goes wrong, usually electrically.

G

BOYS

Gale

Something that will, at best, keep you in your house when you don't want to be there, and at worst destroy it.

Gareth

You rarely hear anyone say they love their name. This will guarantee it.

Garth

Gareth after hitting a wall.

Gary

Gareth after hitting exactly half a can of lager.

Geoffrey

Build your own sex offender.

Giles

Miles and *Niles'* cousin from the country.

Glen

A small valley. The sort of place you'd dump an old fridge.

Gordon

Gordon't.

Graham

Perfect for the son who reminds you of grey ham.

Griffin

Something with the body of a lion, the wings of an eagle and the name of a twat.

Guy

Like calling your child, Child.

H

BOYS

Hal

What the hal.

Harlan

Can you shout this across a park without sounding like a Southern belle who's missing a butler? Haaabsolutely nawt.

Harley

If your surname sounds like Davidson then at least this is funny. Otherwise you may as well just call him Inmate 305834729 and save time.

Harold

*Harold*s are born wearing a hat with a little helicopter blade on and licking a giant lollipop. They never move out of home.

Harrison

This is your opportunity to give your child a different name to every single one of his male classmates. You're blowing it.

Harry

Why is Harry an acceptable name but Barry isn't? There you go, this one's ruined now.

Hector

Verb. To bully.

Herb

US slang. A nerd.

Heston

It's a bad idea to give your child a name made famous by one person, especially a chef.

Holt

Who goes there?

Huck

Huck off.

Hudson

A filthy river.

Hugo

A name so posh it married its own cousin. Why don't Hu-go away and have a think about this one.

Hunter

If you name your child Hunter and he ends up shooting a cat with a crossbow you only have yourself to blame.

I

BOYS

Iago

The Spanish and Welsh version of *James*. Perfect if you want to call your kid *James* but also want them to have to spell it out each time they tell someone.

Ian

A name that really hasn't earned its two syllables.

Iggy

See *Ziggy*.

Ignatius

Grotesque character in *A Confederacy of Dunces*. Grotesque name in *Every Baby Name (Ruined)*.

Ike

What your grandma yells when she sees a mouse in the pantry.

Ira

Naming your son after a proscribed terrorist group in the United States and the United Kingdom might mean they get held up at the airport. Plus, they'll have to do something pretty big to get onto the first page of Google.

Isaac

It's craap.

Ivan

Apple's latest commercial vehicle.

Iwan

Contraction/abbreviation of 'I want to divorce my parents, like Macaulay Culkin did.'

J

BOYS

Jack

Jack shit, *Jack* off, *Jack* my sack, and so on and so forth.

Jackson

Jacksoff.

Jagger

Jagger, Jagger, elderly shagger.

Jai

The ur-bogan.

Jake

Old-fashioned hip hop slang for a policeman. Like calling a child *Plod* or *Filth*.

James

A big *Jamie*.

Jamie

A tiny *James*.

Jared

Disgraced Subway spokesman.

Jasper

A type of rock. And not even a useful one.

Jaxon

Jackson after two cans of energy drink.

Jaxxon

Three cans.

Jayden

See also *Brayden*, *Kayden*, *Rayden*.

Jazz

They say *Jazz* is about the notes you don't play. In this case it's about a name you don't give your kid. If you're really committed to naming your son *Jazz* you should at least write it like JaZz or J a z z or something.

Jet

You're betting on your child being sleek, fast and cool. And not used to carry questionable businessmen to a private island.

Jimmy

US slang. Condom.

Joffrey

It's easy to say the name *Joffrey* was killed off by the *Game of Thrones* character but he only put the final drop of hemlock in the mead, so to speak.

John

Noun. (US). A man who visits prostitutes.
Noun. (US). A toilet.

Johnny

UK slang. Condom.

Johnson

US slang. Cock. 'If I'd had a *Johnny* on my *Johnson*, Johnny, you and Johnson wouldn't be around.'

Jonah

Apocryphal sailor who hasn't had the ridicule he deserves. How stupid do you have to be to end up in the belly of a whale? They eat plankton for fucks sake.

Jory

Something everybody wants to avoid being in front of, or involved with at all.

Josh

One of those sounds that comes out when a villain hits Batman.

Julian

A foppish antique salesman who smells of old books, and not in a good way.

Junior

All babies are *Junior*. This is really fucking lazy.

Jye

See *Jai*.

K

BOYS

Kaden

See *Brayden*, *Aiden*, *Jayden*.

Karl

See *Carl*.

Keith

A name that manages to smell weird. Like wet newspaper and bad dreams.

Kelvin

A unit of measurement, like *foot* and *milligram*.

Kennedy

A man who, despite being the most protected person in the world, managed to get shot in the head in public, in the middle of the day, in his car. Even Donald Trump didn't do that. Let's stop celebrating mediocrity.

Kenneth

Olde Englishe word meaning 'boringe bastarde'.

Kenny

A feeble attempt to make *Kenneth* cool.

Kevin

You can't yell this without sounding like the mum from *Home Alone*.

Klay

If you're going to name your son after a sludgy mass at least have the guts to spell it properly. See *Clay*.

Kolt

See *Colt*.

L

BOYS

Lance

Noun. Something you stab people with. Long and thin. Technologically surpassed by *Gun, Tank,* etc.

Larry

See *Harry.*

Lawrence

There has never been a *Lawrence* who could both swim and ride a bike.

Leonard

Old English word meaning 'he who saves old newspapers in piles until they block out all light into his living room'.

Leonardo

Italian word meaning 'he who saves old newspapers in piles until they block out all light into his living room'.

Leroy

Possibly from the French for 'the king' but more likely from the French for 'the Roy'.

Lester

Lester we forget that other names are available.

Levi

The jeans your uncle wears when there's a band on at the RSL.

Lewie

When you want to call your child *Louis* but are worried it doesn't look stupid enough.

Lewis

See *Louis*.

Lincoln

Former US president with the second-most twattish hat.

Lloyd

Hey! Save some Ls for the rest of us!

Louis

Get him ready for a lifetime of people asking "Is it *Loo-ee*, like the French king? Or *Loo-is*, like loo and piss?"

Lucas

Luke not good enough for you?

Lucien

Will insist on something like a harp or a lute for his eighth birthday.

Luke

A name from the Bible that looks like it's in there by accident.

M

BOYS

Maddox

Eighties-movie-villain-ass name.

Mal

French for 'bad'.

Malcolm

Call your baby *Malcolm* and he's going to come out older than you. Like 20 years older.

Marc

French for *Mark*.

Marcus

Roman for *Marc*.

Mark

Noun. A rube, an idiot. Gullible. But you're going to be the one giving him free lunches for 18 years.

Marshall

If you like Eminem this much you should not have children.

Martin

A name so bland you will forget it immediately. Fine if you want to call your child 'mate' until one of you moves out.

Marvin

Marvin Gaye was shot by his dad. We don't know if it was because he was called *Marvin*, but we don't know if it wasn't, either.

Mason

Mason literally means 'builder'. Consider *Foreman*, they earn more. Or *I.T Consultant*.

Matthew

Another anachronistic Bible name, like *Luke*. It's hard to imagine a man from 5 BC called Matthew. All the *Ezekiel*s and *Malachi*s were probably pretty shitty to him about it.

Max

Fine if your surname is Smith, not if it's Sentence.

Melvin

Old Anglo-Saxon name meaning 'stay 200 metres away from schools, parks and other places children congregate.'

Michael

Average name, average childhood, average job, average life.

Mick

Sure, he'll fix your car by the time he's twelve. He'll also steal the catalytic converter.

Miles

See *Myles*.

Milo

Imagine a grown-up called *Milo*.

Mitchell

There's a 50/50 chance every *Mitchell* will either play sport for Australia, or be caught on camera crashing their Ford Falcon into a telegraph pole for the insurance money. Roll the dice.

Mo

Mo-tion sickness, mo-lester, and so on.

Monty

Quirky, like poking your own eye out so you can wear a cool eyepatch.

Myles

See *Miles*.

N

BOYS

Nathaniel

Are you having a boy or a girl? Neither, you're having the ghost of an 1850s whaling captain.

Nelson

Was the first person you thought of the South African president or the bully from *The Simpsons*? Be honest.

Niles

Miles' nemesis. Like Mario and Wario if they were accountants instead of plumbers.

Noah

Biblical boat builder. Noah got two of every animal on board to save them from the flood, which means he is personally responsible for wasps, tiger snakes, magpies and jellyfish.

Noam

Noam Chomsky is a famous linguist and philosopher. Your kid won't be.

Norman

Neither beast, nor man.

Nigel

'Little baby Nigel.' Preposterous.

Nixon

Almost palindromic former US president who was categorically NOT impeached and therefore NOT a crook.

O

BOYS

Oakley

Those sunglasses modern day war criminals wear.

Odin

Norse god of poetry and magic. Hope you like home-made birthday presents.

Odyn

See *Odin*.

Odysseus

See *Ulysses*.

Oliver

Derived from the Latin word for 'olive tree planter'. Great.

Opie

No hopie.

Orion

Unremarkable Ford car criticised for its tedious design.

Orson

A lovely way to let people know you appreciate classic cinema, but have no idea about the cruelty of children.

Orville

Awful.

Oscar

Something people are losing interest in at an exponential rate.

Oswald

Famous British fascist. Look it up.

Ozzy

A colloquial term for an Australian person. Like all nationality-based names, walks the line between very goofy and slightly racist.

P

BOYS

Palmer

Euphemism for masturbator.

Parker

English for valet.

Patrick

Two classic uncle names smashed together to make one unexceptional nephew name.

Paul

The only name that was in the Bible, the Beatles and the list of children most likely to bring a dead cat to school.

Paxton

The perfect name for one of those kids that is older than his uncle. You know the ones. Can drive by the time they're six.

Payne

That thing we all try and avoid.

Percy

Adj. Something that looks a bit like a purse.

Peter

Noun. US slang for cock, penis.

Phineas

The butler in a story about a man and his idiot butler. How a cockney says 'thin ears'.

Piers

Those long things seagulls shit on.

Pike

One of the most unpleasant fish, which, let's be honest, are already a disagreeable type of creature.

Presley

See *Elvis*.

Prince

But which one? *Prince* the dead singer, balding and irrelevant *Prince* William of England, or Martin *Prince*, the bothersome wet blanket from *The Simpsons*.

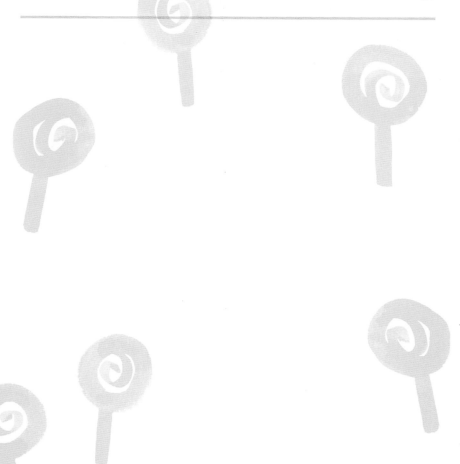

Q

BOYS

Quentin

A word that sounds like a
tiny amount of something.
'I only have a quentin of
sympathy for his parents.
After all, they were the ones
who named him *Quentin* and we
all read the manifesto in the
newspaper.'

Quinton

Drunk *Quentin*.

R

BOYS

Ralph

Verb. US slang for vomiting.

Ramsay

See *Heston*.

Randall

Randy with his trousers back on.

Randy

Noun. Horny, but in a uniquely off-putting, British way.

Rider

Nondescript American horseshit.

Robert

Robert Hansen was an unspeakably cruel American serial killer, and *Robert* just isn't a good enough name to ignore this.

Rocky

A fictional, semi-literate punching bag, and a classic name for a dangerous dog.

Roger

What elderly British men call fucking.

Roland

If you ever lose *Roland* you can find him with his nose pressed up against a confectioner's window somewhere.

Roman

Another name which, somehow, sounds a little bit 'nothing wrong with being proud of my white heritage'. See *Arya*, *Ozzy*.

Romeo

Fictional dead man who disgraced his family and caused a whole lot of other trouble.

Rory

Local football club mascot, if their crest features a lion or a rotund private schoolboy.

Ross

Deafeningly unremarkable.

Rowan

Yet another type of tree. Do you expect your son to look like a tree?

Rupert

Boys called *Rupert* will expect you to find a wife for them, preferably one of good stock and from a reputable family, before spending the rest of their days attending to their maladies in a darkened room.

Rusty

Descriptive of something that might give you tetanus.

Ryder

See *Rider*.

S

BOYS

Sage

A common herb, the smoke from which is thought to dispel evil spirits — cough *bullshit* cough. At some point *Sage* will be picked up and waved about by an old lady with beads in her hair. Possibly with his feet on fire.

Sam

See *Samuel*.

Samuel

Call a kid *Samuel* and you're ending up with either a lighthouse keeper or the caretaker for a haunted factory. Not good.

Sandy

Please don't name your child after the most annoying thing they can be.

Saul

A small *Paul*.

Sawyer

Noun. Someone who cuts wood for a living. Not much call for that these days.

Sebastian

Sebastian is an anagram of 'Beatin' ass', 'A sin beast' and 'I stab Sean', which is ironic given its impossibly craven look and sound.

Seth

The sound an angry cat makes.

Shea

Sheat.

Silas

Every little *Silas* is born with dungarees, a frayed straw hat and a gallon jug with XXX on.

Sol

A bad beer and a worse name.

Stanley

Something people used to be called, back before we knew about better names.

T

BOYS

Tag

Not it.

Teddy

Twee bullshit for parents who wear flat caps and drink flavoured gin.

Terry

A career selling fruit and vegetables from a market stall beckons. Hope you like bananas!

Theodore

Long for *Teddy* (see above). Twee bullshit for parents who buy slightly more expensive flat caps and flavoured gin.

Thierry

Une carrière dans la vente de fruits et légumes sur un étal de marché attends. J'espère que vous aimez les bananes!

Thomas

This means 'twin' in Greek. Is your child a twin? No? Don't call him Thomas. Yes? Congratulations! Call them both Thomas.

Timothee

You'vee got to bee kidding mee.

Timothy

Like polio and manners, *Timothy* has almost been eradicated among young children. Calling your child *Timothy* could set us back years.

Tobin

A handy name that also describes where it should go.

Toby

Adj. 'Sorry I gave you such an awful name, I'd just been in labour for 16 hours and was feeling a bit toby.'

Topher

Shit for 'Christopher'.

Travis

After the homicidal taxi driver, or the homicidal chimp?

Trey

Something your grandmother eats dinner off when her quiz show is on the TV.

Trip

Verb. To fall over. Or hallucinate from drugs. Or fall over while hallucinating from drugs.

Tristan

The straw boater and pulled-up socks of names. Friends with *Toby*.

Tucker

Just trying to think
whether this rhymes
with anything. Give me a
minute.[1]

Tyler

Start practising the
phrases 'He was framed';
'It was almost a
victimless crime'; 'That
judge never liked him
since he was eleven'.

[1]Fucker

U

BOYS

Ulric

Possibly Swedish for *Rick*, definitely English for 'kid who likes dragons a concerning amount'.

Ulysses

Ulysses (*Odysseus* in Greek) took ten years to cover a journey of 500 miles. When he got home he told his wife it was because of sea monsters, and other such things. I think we can see what kind of man he was.

Unique

Funny if there are two of these in his class. Otherwise, no.

Uriel

Sounds medical.

Utah

Probably the most boring state in America. No one goes on holiday to *Utah*. Even the Mormons are putting on a brave face.

V

BOYS

Valentine

A 'holiday' invented by a greetings card company to sell plush teddy bears and make ugly people feel bad. You don't even get the day off.

Valiant

Synonym for 'brave', which is what you have to be if your name is *Valiant*.

Vance

One of those names that sounds like it was made by an algorithm.

Vaughan

Yawaghn.

Victor

Synonym for 'winner', which technically he is as he reached the egg first. Call your child *Victor* and you can be reminded of that corporeal process every time you hear it.

Virgil

A famous Roman poet, and a character from Thunderbirds. Nerd shit, basically.

W

BOYS

Walker

A metal frame geriatrics use so they don't fall down on their way to buy their eighth property.

Walter

Sounds like a cockney saying 'water'.

Watson

Not much, what's on with you?

Wendal

A homeless man from an Arrested Development song.

Wendell

A sickly child from *The Simpsons*.

Wendill

A made up name from a book about what not to call your baby.

Wesley

Wesley comes from the Old English meaning 'field to the west'. To the west of what? It doesn't even make sense. Enjoy your random field kid.

William

If you name your child *William* you are also naming them *Bill*, *Billy*, *Willy*, Will and potentially *Liam*. There's too much that could go wrong.

Winston

A porcine racist.

Wolfgang

A gang of wolves isn't even called a wolf gang. It's called a pack. Would you name your child *Pack*? You probably would, wouldn't you.

Woodson

What they would call the Pinocchio character in an unlicensed remake.

Woody

US slang. An erection.

Wrangler

Not as good as *Levi*.

X

BOYS

Xander

What people called *Alexander* tell people their name is in their first year of uni.

Xavier

How do you even pronounce this? Zavier? Ksavier? Havier? Xaven't got a clue.

Xenon

Prop. noun. A type of gas. Dense, but odourless.

Y

BOYS

Yago
See *Iago*.

Yuri
A famous Russian cosmonaut and a word that sounds like you're going mad when you shout it.

Yves
Not so much a name as a collection of letters.

Z

BOYS

Zachary

See *Zack*.

Zack

Nut*zack*.

Zander

See *Xander*.

Zane

In*zane*.

Zephyr

Noun. Literally wind. Consider also *Gust*, *Flatulence*.

Zeus

The Greek god of thunder, *Zeus* was so upset about human sacrifices he tried to kill everybody in the world. He also fucked his sister. Pro-death penalty for murder, pro-incest … Are we sure he wasn't from Arkansas?

Ziggy

Remember that your son will have to introduce himself to people.

A

GIRLS

Abigail

Imagine people's disappointment when they think they're getting 'a big ale' and have to meet your kid instead.

Adalyn

One baby? Or two old ladies?

Addison

Because you wish you 'ad a son?

Adelaide

A city known for its preponderance of serial killers.

Aileen

Aileen Wuornos had a terrible life before becoming a notorious murderer. There's a lot of nuance in her case, so let's err on the side of caution and fuck this one off.

Ailsa

Ancient northern European word meaning 'elf victory'. Modern Australian word meaning 'old lady from *Home and Away*'.

Ainsley

See *Ainslie*.

Ainslie

A name that somehow seems ashamed of itself.

Alana

Would you call your son *Alan*? If so, this is the name for you. Anagram of *Aanal*, but at least that one would be first on the class register.

Alexa

The name that launched a thousand devices, *Alexa* is the perfect name for a small, hard, grey cylindrical child. Try shouting it in JB HiFi and see what happens.

Alice

It's just 'lice' or 'a louse'.

Amanda

From the Latin meaning 'you deserve to be loved', which is what you say to someone when nobody loves them.

Angel

Why not name your daughter after an infallible divine being? No pressure.

April

Just a nothing month.

Areola

Sure. Why not. How did you even get this far?

Aretha

Phonetically close to 'urethra'. (That's your piss hole.)

Arya

Force everyone to guess whether you are a *Game of Thrones* obsessive or a racist simply by naming your child *Arya*. Either way, nobody will want to sit next to you at parents evening.

Ashlee

Sporty Ashley

Ashlei

Scary Ashley

Ashleigh

Posh Ashley

Ashli

Baby Ashley

Ashlii

Ginger Ashley

Ashlynn

Out of the womb with a perfectly coiffed blonde bob and a Kentucky accent. Start saving for the horse now.

Asia

When you can't decide between *India* and *Papua New Guinea*.

Astra

One of the least exciting car brand's least exciting cars.

Aubree

Aw no.

Ava

Only good if your surname is Cado, and actually that's stopped being funny before the end of this sentence.

Avery

This is where birds live.

Avril

French for *April*. Sounds a bit like anvil.

B

GIRLS

Bailey

Noun. Castle wall. That thing every young girl wants to be compared to.

Barbara

It's honestly cool you don't care that much about this whole naming thing.

Beatrix

Sounds like knock-off LEGO.

Belinda

No, be anyone else.

Bella

Italian for 'beautiful', which is pretty fucking arrogant.

Belle

Belle Gunness was an American serial killer from the late 19th century. She would lure men with the promise of marriage, then kill them. Imagine how efficient she'd have been with Facebook.

Bentley

A car coveted by arseholes.

Beth

The Hebrew word for 'house'. Something we are told we want and then drains all our money for the rest of our lives.

Betty

Adj. The behaviour of someone who likes gambling. 'You're very betty today. Did you remember to buy nappies?'

Bianca

Bianca comes from the Italian word for 'white'. Perfect for when you want to seem racist *and* worldly. See *Arya*.

Billie

See *Billy*.

Blythe

Homophonous ('blithe') word meaning happy and carefree but in a selfish, stupid way.

Brandy

If you're going to name your kid after an alcoholic drink, pick a better one than the bottle that's been in your cupboard since grandma died.

Bree

You can't bree serious.

Brenda

See *Nancy*.

Briane

Brian, but a lady.

Briar

Noun. A horrible, thorny bush.

Bridget

You don't hear of many *Bridget*s these days. Probably because it sounds like a hairstyle from the 1950s.

Bridgette

As above but in France.

Brie

'Why did we name you *Brie*? Well, we always loved the name, plus when you get hot you stink of ammonia.'

Briony

A type of plant that you would have heard about by now if it was any good.

Britney

There is one person people will think of every time they hear this name. Former US Big Brother contestant Britney Haynes.

Brooke

From the noun 'brook', meaning a small, gentle stream. Like what grandad has when he has to get up in the night.

Brooklyn

Calling your child *Brooklyn* lets people know you think you know what they think is cool.

Bunty

You know why not.

C

GIRLS

Cairo

Officially the most polluted city in the world.

Callie

A classic name for an old sheepdog.

Camilla

Royal stepmother tolerated by the United Kingdom and largely ignored by the rest of the world. Children have to be told who she is by the teacher before she comes into their classroom, and she still wears a name badge for photo-op factory visits.

Cara

Phonetically identical to the Arabic word for 'shit'. Luckily there are only 315 million people who will notice.

Carleigh

Sureleigh not. See *Carly*.

Carly

Someone who looks a bit like *Carl*.

Carmen

Sounds exotic but really it's a portmanteau of two very common things. So don't try and trick people.

Carolina

Carolina is a contraction of 'Carol in a shit new name'.

Cat

The most spiteful pet money can buy.

Catherine

Catherine the Great was one of those 'boss bitch' royals who had multiple partners and killed a lot of peasants. Now it's something middle-aged Geography teachers are called.

Celia

What they would call the feminine-voiced Artificial Intelligence in a film about a very drab and boring feminine-voiced Artificial Intelligence.

Chanel

A name like *Chanel* lets people know one thing — your child is as precious to you as a bottle of perfume. And that's beautiful.

Chardonnay

The wine that people who say they like wine but really mean they like getting pissed drink.

Charli

You don't have to pay by the letter. See *Charlie*.

Charlie

Slang for cocaine, which is apt as children are not only incredibly expensive but lead to poor sleep and increased irritability.

Charlotte

Royal-sounding, like *Elizabeth* or *Herod*.

Claudia

The lady version of *Claude*, whatever that is.

Clementine

Round and orange.

Cleo

A cat food brand.

Clover

Poisonous to horses.

Colby

Australia's sixth-favourite cheese.

Constance

Unless you are giving birth to the ghost of an 18th-century housekeeper choose something else.

Coral

Will cut your feet.

Crystal

Extremely fragile, but loved by geriatrics and hippies.

D

GIRLS

Daenerys

Only worth it so you can pretend you've never heard of *Game of Thrones* when people ask. Actually, it's still not worth it.

Dahlia

A type of flower. Particularly susceptible to fungal disease.

Danielle

See *Daniel*.

Daphne

In Greek mythology, *Daphne*'s father was called Peneus. Your children are going to give you enough shit in your lifetime, please don't give them free ammunition.

Darlene

Impossible to say without sounding like a nervous Texan husband addressing his rambunctious wife.

Dawn

The thing new parents look forward to the least.

Dayton

The sixth largest city in Ohio. A place that looks incredibly boring.

Debbie

They say everything comes back into fashion, but *Debbie* won't.

Dee

A shit grade, slang for a cock and, when written like this, a complete waste of letters.

Deirdre

From the Gaelic meaning 'sorrowful', which is what we all want for our children, isn't it?

Delilah

'Why, why, why, Delilah?' is what your daughter's first words will be if you name her *Delilah*.

Delta

A pile of sediment found at the mouth of a river. Delightful.

Destiny

It's a great use of irony calling your child *Destiny*, and thus severely limiting theirs. So points for that, I guess.

Devine

How an old lady describes the feeling of putting her feet in hot water, or the taste of sponge cake.

Devon

Cheap ham.

Diana

Formerly the people's princess, now mainly seen on commemorative tea towels.

Diane

From the Persian meaning 'supplier of wellness'. So, 'pharmacist' then. Or 'drug dealer'.

Dido

Milquetoast British singer.
Very close to 'dildo'.

Dior

See *Chanel*.

Diva

Someone that makes
unreasonable demands and
generally annoys everybody
around them. More than a
normal child, even.

Dixie

A word with troubling racial
connotations, given its
history with America's south.
Plus, you know. 'Dicksie'.

Dolores

This is the sort of thing
you call a fishing vessel,
not a girl.

Dominique

See *Dominic*.

Donna

Italian for 'woman'. Imagine
yelling WOMAN across the
house. Sounds disrespectful,
doesn't it?

Doris

Doris comes from the Greek
meaning 'gift of the ocean'.
Flotsam, then.

Dream

Something your co-workers
don't want to hear about.

E

GIRLS

Edith

When you say *Edith* it sounds like you're trying to say 'Ediss' and getting it wrong. But 'Ediss' isn't a name. So that's confusing.

Eileen

See *Aileen*.

Eleanor

*Eleanor*s are the children who remind the teacher when they've forgotten to set homework and, no, this is not a good thing.

Elise

What you take out on a car when you don't have the cash to buy it up front.

Elizabeth

See *Victoria*.

Elle

'ell of a dreary name.

Ellery

What you yell while pointing at your throat when you're choking on celery.

Elsa

Choose something elsa.

Elsie

Choose something elsie.

Ember

Don't be surprised when she burns your house down.

Emerald

You don't see many rom-com actresses being proposed to with an *Emerald* ring. Still better than *Jade*, though.

Emmy

Not as good as *Oscar.*

Erica

The female version of *Eric*. Exotic!

Erika

The female version of *Erik*. As above!

Erin

A little elf's name. *Erin*s all live together in a hollow tree stump, occasionally floating downstream on a big leaf to go foraging for mushrooms. Vulnerable to frost and dogs.

Esmeralda

Anagram of 'Real Damsel'! And 'Medal Arse'.

Essence

Noun. Smell, stench, etc.

Esther

Pronounced 'Ester', so why not fucking spell it like that.

Ethel

Sure, *Ethel*s are usually tiny
and wrinkled, and smell of
piss. But they're also usually
80 years old.

Etta

Do betta.

Evangeline

Anagram of 'An evil gene'.

Eve

The other one (see *Adam*)
who fucked it for everybody,
if you believe the Bible.
If it wasn't for *Eve* we'd
all be living in a nice
garden, stark bollock naked
and eating (or not eating?)
apples.

F

GIRLS

Faith

See *Grace*.

Fallon

Help, I've *Fallon* down and I can't get up.

Fanny

See *Areola*.

Fawn

A baby deer and a word meaning to act obsequiously.

Felicity

From the Latin meaning 'good luck', which, with a name that sounds like that, they will need.

Fern

Just a regular type of plant. Nothing special.

Fifi

Perfect … for a POODLE.

Fleur

Eurgh.

Flora

Collective noun. Plants and trees, etc. Roses, daisies and daffodils, but also venus fly-traps and those ones that smell like a dead body.

Florence

A city in Italy full of the Contiki tourists that delude themselves they're better than the others. The female version of *Lawrence*, possibly.

Frankie

Wanky.

Freja

See *Freya*.

Freya

Another Norse goddess name, *Freya* is associated with sex and fertility. Pretty weird thing to call a baby, then, isn't it? What's wrong with you?

G

GIRLS

Gabby

Adj. Descriptive of somebody who never shuts the fuck up.

Gabrielle

Adj. Descriptive of somebody who never shuts the fuck up about the time they went to Italy after uni.

Gazelle

Frequently eaten by lions.

Georgina

Female version of George.
Latin: 'George with a vagina'.

Ginny

Adj. Smells like gin.

Gloria

Morning *Gloria*, *Gloria* hole, there are more.

Grace

Insipid abstract noun.
The naming version of buying someone a birthday present on the way to the party.

Greta

Gret a fucking clue.

Gretchen

Sounds like a word Scottish people would use for 'complaining'. 'Stop gretchen and eat your meat sock. What are you, English?'

Guinevere

Guinevere is a real 'statement' name, the statement being that we are far too into movies about wizards and we don't care if it ruins our daughter's life.

Gwendolyn

See *Guinevere*.

H

GIRLS

Hailey

More bad weather. See *Gale*.

Haley

See *Hailey*.

Halo

Is it me you're looking for?

Hannah

Ha! Nah.

Harmony

How can one thing be *Harmony*? *Harmony* with what? The cognitive dissonance makes you feel like you're having a stroke when you concentrate on it.

Heather

See *Briar*.

Heidi

Popularised by the classic Swiss story about a little girl who lived in the mountains with her grandparents. The fact this book took off says more about the state of Swiss literature than it does about the name *Heidi*.

Helen

Helen of Troy was said to be the most beautiful woman in the world. She'd probably only be like a 6 or a 7 today, though.

Helga

Perfect for the bread-shaped baby.

Henrietta

The sort of thing an upper-middle class family would name one of their chickens.

Hettie

Another one of those 'better for dogs' names. This one would go well with a Labrador, or perhaps a King Charles Spaniel.

Holiday

Naming your child *Holiday* is a nice way to remember something you used to do.

Holly

Poisonous bush.

Honey

Bee shit.

Honour

Do you really want your daughter's name tattooed on thousands of bogans and infantrymen before she's even born?

Hope

See *Grace*.

Hyacinth

Hiya, lifetime of woe.

GIRLS

Ida

Unless this is being passed down through your family, don't do it. If it is, this is your chance to be a hero and end it.

Ilana

Vaguely Russian sounding, but we're talking Siberian peasant not Bond villainess.

Imogen

Imogen all the puns.

India

You wear those baggy trousers you get from a stall in Thailand, yeah? But only on the weekend? You used to have a nose ring until you got a job in an office? You're having a water birth, right? You have a 'doula'?

Indie

A way to describe music that not very many people like.

Indigo

Purple with a stupid hat on.

Iris

One of the stickiest body parts.

Isabel

No, is a baby.

Isabella

What an Italian person says when they think they've seen a bell.

Isadora

What an Italian person says
when they think they've seen
a door.

Isla

Names with a silent letter
are deceitful. Let's be honest
about the whole thing.

Isolde

From the old German word for
'ice', the drug that will
either ruin your life or make
you want to do the dishes.

Ita

It a bad name.

Ivana

See *Ilana*.

Ivy

Irritating.

J

GIRLS

Jade

A semi-precious name for your semi-precious daughter.

Jamie

Popular with parents who have those family portrait photos up in the lounge.

Jane

Offensively plain.

Janet

Small *Jane*.

Janette

Small, bogan *Jane*.

Jasmine

The last box of tea in the office cupboard.

Jayde

What's wrong with *Jade?* Oh, that's right.

Jewel

When you want to signal that your child is valuable in a vague, unspecified way.

Joanne

Putting two dull names together doesn't make one good one. It's like multiplying a negative. Remember, from maths? Of course you don't, you almost named your kid *Joanne.*

Jolene

This will always remind people of that one song, 'The Baby With The Shitty Name'.

Joni

People will pronounce it *Johnny* and you can't blame them.

Journey

A word that means something more than 'commute' but less than 'holiday'. What celebrities go on after they've been caught with a bag of *Charlie* and want to get back on TV.

Julie

Julie comes from the Latin for 'youthful'. All babies are youthful. You may as well call her 'hungry', or 'annoying' or 'loud'.

Justine

Just don't.

K

GIRLS

Kaci

Kacky? Cassie? Catchy?

Karen

The good: *Karen* is back!
The bad: *Karen* is now a
catch-all term for an
annoying bitch.

Karma

Something you have to be
permanently afraid of.

Kashmir

A disputed territory. Perfect
for when you get divorced.

Katelynn

2021's least anticipated
mash-up.

Katherine

See *Catherine*.

Kaylee

When something tastes a bit like kale.

Kenna

Kenn a get a 'hell no'.

Kensington

A suburb of Melbourne famous for its abattoir. Not famous, exactly.

Kenzie

Mackenzie for those people for whom three syllables is just too ostentatious.

Kristina

Mildly amusing if the parents are called *Kris* and *Tina*. Mildly.

Krystal

Originally a registrar's mistake. See *Crystal*.

Krystel

Don't make it worse.

Krystle

Pys off.

L

GIRLS

Lacy

Things that can be lacy
include bras, dresses and
the veins in your leg when
there's something wrong.
Things that cannot be lacy
include your daughter.

Lana

See *Alan*.

Laura

Laura comes from the Latin
for bay laurel. That's the
gross, shitty leaf you forget
to take out of your casserole
before eating it.

Lauren

Every single *Lauren* has an
annoying voice, and no one
knows why.

Layla

Forever associated with
Eric Clapton, who is forever
associated with making
questionable remarks about
immigration.

Leah

Barely even a word, this
is the sound you make the
morning after three bottles
of wine.

Liberty

Enormous green lady covered
in bird shit.

Lily

What posh women call their
vagina.

Lizbeth

Hipster relic of the 1800s.

Lola

A contraction of 'lol another set of parents who think they're unique and quirky'.

London

Knife crime capital of Europe.

Lou

The female version of *John*, in that it is slang for 'toilet'.

Louisa

Can be shortened to *Lou*.

Louise

See above.

Lucinda

Lucy with an art history degree.

Lucy

Lucinda with a Certificate 1 in graphic design.

Luna

From the Latin meaning 'moon'. Great if you anticipate your daughter being distant and pale.

Lyric

Which one? 'I love you baby,
and if it's quite alright I
need you baby?' Or 'Fuck you
I won't do what you tell me,
fuck you I won't do what you
tell me?'

Lysette

A wonderful name for a brand
of insecticide.

M

GIRLS

Maddison

The Live, Laugh, Love decorative wooden sign of names.

Maddisyn

As above but it's Live, Laugh, Love, Lose Your Phone At A Hens Party.

Maeve

Maeve is an ancient Irish word meaning 'she who intoxicates'. Alternatives include *Tooheys*, *Coolabah*, *Glass Barbecue* and *Glue*.

Malaya

This isn't a name — it's what your racist uncle calls Malaysia.

Mandy

What happens to *Amandas* when they turn 40.

Marion

Marions are born with glasses on a chain around their neck and a job in a library. Too easy to confuse with *Marlon*.

Marley

We get it, you smoke weed.

Mary

Congratulations! It's a spinster!

Meagan

Popular even though nobody knows whether to pronounce this *Meggan* or *Meegan*. Save us all the hassle and choose something else.

Megan

See *Meagan*.

Meghan

See *Megan*.

Meggan

Fuck off.

Melania

Before Donald Trump, *Melania* was just a name that sounded a bit like skin cancer. Now it's shorthand for a money-grabbing, fascist-adjacent waste of atoms.

Melena

Noun. A black, tarry stool. And not the kind you sit on.

Melissa

Mel is a what? Haha, but seriously, this name sucks.

Melody

[Tips stripper who gave you the idea.]

Me'lody

[Tips fedora.]

Mel'ody

[Tips self into oncoming traffic.]

Mercedes

After the car? Congratulations on your 1200kg, German daughter.

Mia

Fun game — go to any playpark, shout 'Baby Mia's dropped her cigarettes!' and watch thirty mums with neck tattoos turn around.

Moll

Moll Cutpurse was a notorious petty criminal. That might sound cool, but today's equivalent is a girl who steals from 7-Eleven so much she gets in the newspaper. Only now she's got a stupid old-fashioned name.

Molly

Slang for MDMA.

Monica

The most annoying character in *Friends*, which is really, really saying something.

Monroe

'Please don't name your baby after me. I didn't even say most of those things you see on Facebook with my name and a date underneath' (Marilyn Monroe, 1961).

Morgan

Fine if you want it to sound like the Swedish Chef named your baby.

Morwenna

Ancient Cornish word meaning 'arsehole parents'.

N

GIRLS

Nadia

Sounds like a drunk person saying 'no idea'.

Nancy

This is the sort of name you give to a haunted doll. See also *Brenda*.

Nanette

A tiny nan.

Naomi

Create your own curly haired, twice divorced high school art teacher with a discreet tattoo and eight pairs of different coloured sandals simply by naming your child *Naomi*.

Natasha

From the Russian meaning 'born at Christmas'. A nice way to remind yourself roughly when to buy a birthday present. Ironically, 'Ah satan' backwards.

Ness

See *Nessie.*

Nessie

Affectionate name for the enormous sea monster that lives in Loch Ness, which is a weird thing to give an affectionate name to.

Nevaeh

In the 1950s you would be put in an institution and forced to drink holy water for saying 'Heaven' backwards. Now you just get weird looks from the grandparents.

Nina

Noun (Spanish). Little girl. If you call her this she's going to know you forgot to choose a name and panicked at the last minute.

Noelle

A word meaning 'Christmas, but just for the ladies.' Possibly.

Noni

Another colloquialism for people too shy to say 'vagina'. See *Lily*.

Nora

Meet *Nora*, the incredible 89-year-old baby.

Novah

One of those names that looks like it should mean something backwards, but somehow means even less.

GIRLS

Oaklee

One of those guns-and-horses-
and-marrying-your-nextdoor-
neighbour names you get in
places like Virginia, Kentucky
and Brisbane.

Oaklynn

A good name for a retirement
home.

Ocean

A place that is either
extremely dangerous or
extremely boring.

Odette

Quaint, French-sounding merde
for parents who desperately
want cooler friends.

Olive

Small, bitter. An acquired taste.

Olivia

Sounds like a laxative, or an off-brand butter substitute. Either way she's going to be embarrassing at the supermarket checkout.

Oliviah

Private school *Olivia*.

Olwynne

A good name for a magical owl, a bad name for a human baby.

Oona

You shouldn't name your child after the noises you made while you were giving birth to them.

Ophelia

The first evolution of *Persephone*.

Oriola

See *Areola*.

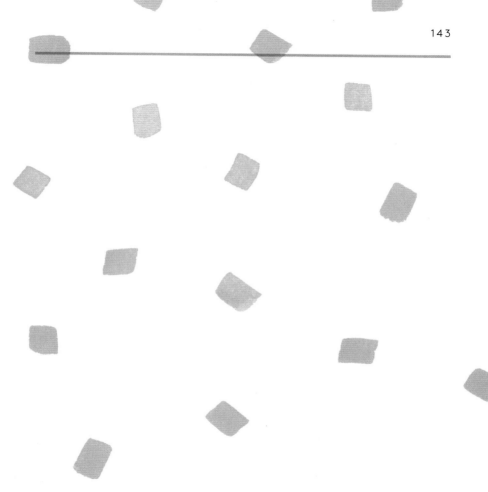

P

GIRLS

Paige

For parents who love literature.

Paisley

We put 1,000 middle-class American white girls names into a computer and this is what came out.

Pam

See *Josh*.

Papua New Guinea

This is honestly no worse than some of the other ideas in here.

Paris

City of love? City of dog shit and overpriced bread.

Patience

The kind of name they were giving out back when the pilgrims landed. Name your child *Patience* and you might as well make her wear a big hat with a buckle on and get a job milking cows.

Patty

Noun. Beefburger.

Pauline

Poor choice.

Paxtyn

We put 1,000 middle-class white American girls names into a computer and something went badly wrong. This is what came out.

Payton

A fictional town in a young adult book about aliens or horses or some crap.

Pearl

Glorified sand.

Peggy

When you have a baby that looks like a peg, well, there's only one name for it. *Peggy* is also short for *Margaret*, as if that makes any fucking sense whatsoever. There isn't even a P in there. (In *Margaret*. There is a P in *Peggy*, right at the beginning.)

Penelope

Persephone's final form. See *Ophelia*.

Penny

The least amount of money you can get.

Perdita

What a mid-range sofa shop would call one of their mid-range sofas.

Persephone

Sounds like a Pokémon.

Peta

The charity that most likes to show you pictures of dead animals.

Petra

One of those dishes you make a disease in.

Petroula

What they call a service station in Greece, probably.

Philippa

Sounds like a minor royal. A very minor royal.

Phoebe

The quirky one in *Friends* i.e 'The One Nobody Wanted To Say Was Them'.

Phoenix

An imaginary bird that's on fire.

Piper

Someone who smokes a pipe.

Pippa

Irredeemably twee.

Polly

Slang for 'politician', that type of person everybody loves.

Poppy

What heroin comes from.

Porsha

Portia with -10 charisma.

Portia

Porsha with -10 fighting ability.

Q

GIRLS

Queenie

What's the most regal name
on the planet? OK, great.
Now make it sound like a
baby is saying it.

Quest

If you're going to name your
daughter after where she was
conceived choose the city, not
the hotel brand.

Quincey

A quince is rock-hard, sour
and pointless. *Quincey* is
something reminiscent of
that.

Quinn

Quinn comes from the Gaelic
word for 'wise'. But babies
know absolutely fuck-all.

R

GIRLS

Raegan

Yet aenother aersehole former president.

Reagan

Yet another arsehole former president.

Regan

Yet nother rsehole former president.

Regena

Sounds like thrush medicine.

Regina

Sounds like where you apply the thrush medicine.

Renee

Doctor, lawyer, veterinarian, you name it. *Renee* will be their foul-tempered receptionist.

Rhea

Dire.

Rhianna

See *Rhiannon*.

Rhianne

See *Rianne*.

Rhiannon

All this time you could have been picking out a nice name for your child.

Rhonda

E Honda is a character in the *Street Fighter* franchise. Honda R is a fast car. *Rhonda* is a cold, grey valley in Wales.

Riane

See *Rhianna*.

Rianne

See *Riane*.

Riley

Really?

Robyn

An Englysh byrd and Batman's useless sydekyck.

Rose

An unimaginative gift from a guilty partner; a woman who would rather let her boyfriend drown than share a floating door with him.

Rosemary

A drab herb.

Rosie

The colour your face goes when you are dehydrated or having a heart attack.

Roxy

Get your porn star name by being called '*Roxy*'.

Ruby

This might make sense to begin with but your baby won't be shiny and red forever.

Ruta

The best — the *best* — you can hope for is that the other kids tease her for sounding like a piece of internet equipment.

Ruth

Scooby Doo's favourite name.

Ryann

Stick another *n* on there, since we're just chucking them around. Have another one. *Ryannnnn*. How about that?

S

GIRLS

Sailor

Yet another 'job' name, this one associated with bad language, profligate sexual practices and, in some countries, people smuggling. Also an open goal for the nickname 'seaman'.

Sally

A name that only exists in children's story books and lists of greyhounds still up for adoption.

Samantha

From the ancient Hebrew meaning 'Woman who yells at her children in the supermarket while wearing pyjamas'.

Scarlett

What you've done there is, you've just spelled a colour wrong. Why not call your kid *Yelloww*? Or *Rod*.

Serena

See *Serenity*.

Serenity

Probably the most ironic name you can give a newborn baby.

Shelby

Shelby living with this name for the rest of her life.

Shyla

There are three life paths available to every *Shyla*. Southern American barmaid, Southern American tour guide, or Southern American barmaid-tour guide

Sierra

Another dreary Ford car. See *Orion*.

Sky

Enormous and unpredictable.

Skye

See *Sky*.

Sophia

Soboring.

Stella

From the Latin for 'star' and the English for 'strong lager that makes you think you can run through a wall'.

Stormie

See *Stormy*.

Stormy

A name that says 'We love you, but we're afraid of you'.

Sunday

The most depressing day of the week.

Susan

Lazy.

T

GIRLS

Tailor

Noun. Someone who makes clothes. Just a job. See *Sailor*, *Mason*.

Tallow

Noun. Beef fat.

Tammy

Short for tampon.

Tamsin

Shortened form of *Thomasina*. So, see *Thomasina*.

Tamsyn

A virtual *Tamsin*.

Tansy

Sounds like a start-up that delivers feminine products to your work within the hour.

Tara

How northern English people say 'goodbye'.

Tasha

See *Natasha*.

Tawny

A type of owl. Don't be surprised when you see her turn her head 360 degrees. Or cough up a rat.

Tayla

A *Tailor* that makes clothes for children who do beauty pageants.

Taylah

A *Tailor* that makes clothes for people who put Playboy stickers in their car windows.

Taylor

A *Tailor* that makes clothes for people who went to private school but pretend they didn't.

Tegan

A name of various origins, all of which seem to mean 'beautiful'. Feeling confident?

Teneale

Ten eel? What is this, a name or an order at the fish market?

Tess

One of those names the sad-sack lady has in old novels about sad-sack ladies. Born to lose.

Tessa

Can't polish a turd. See *Tess*.

Thomasina

See *Thomas*.

Tina

Looks too much like 'tuna'.

Treasure

When a gang of pirates turns up at your house holding a map with an X on it you'll realise your mistake.

Trixie

Sounds like a made-up cat food brand they'd use on a TV show so they don't get in trouble with the makers of *Cleo*.

U

GIRLS

Uma

When you can't choose a
name for your child why not
use the literal sound of
indecision?

Una

See *Oona.*

Unity

See *Harmony.*

Ursula

Underwater Disney villain.

V

GIRLS

Vanity

An incredibly poor trait.
Why is this even a name?

Vanya

Sounds like a threat.
'Step out in the road again
and I'll van ya.'

Venice

Another Italian city, this
time full of boomer tourists
and scam artists. Smells
weird, but they don't put
that in the guidebooks. See
Florence.

Venus

Probably one of the worst
planets, plus it rhymes with
a rude body part (aenus).

Verity

Noun. Word meaning 'true'.
Say 'true' then, Wordsworth.
Stop wasting people's time.

Victoria

See *Charlotte*.

Viola

Something that makes a
terrible sound when combined
with a child.

Violet

See *Indigo*.

Virginia

A state in the US famous for its stupid name and a phenomenal rate of opioid addiction.

Vivian

A judgemental old woman. Like a *Karen* but with more of those neck flaps elderly middle-class complainers seem to get, that flare red when they are aroused.

Vivienne

French *Vivian*. *Avec les neck flaps aussi.*

W

GIRLS

Wendy

A strange little redheaded girl who sells burgers and lives in a tiny house in your garden.

Wiley

Adj. Sly, deceitful.

Willow

A type of depressed tree.

Winnie

The sound of a frightened horse.

Winona

From the Latin meaning 'light-fingered thespian'.

Winter

The shittest season.

Wren

Wren are you going to choose a better name?

X

GIRLS

Xandra

'We named you after where you were conceived.' (Backseat of what might be a mid-market Korean hatchback.)

Xena

A fictional, but still very violent, woman.

Xenia

What a nine year old would name a planet in their story about aliens.

Xoe

Zoe for parents who think they're special or something. Looks a little too much like 'Hoe'.

Y

GIRLS

Yanet
Ya better not.

Yasmin
See *Jasmine*.

Yasmine
See *Jasmine*.

Yolanda
Yolanda yourself.

Z

GIRLS

Zelda

A good way to tell people you are obsessed with video games, although it's usually already pretty obvious.

Zilla

What babies and atheists call Godzilla.

Zina

See *Xena*.

Zoe

Another name that arrogantly takes two syllables when it only deserves one. See *Ian*.

Zora

Exists in that vanishingly thin crossover of old lady and stinking hippy, somehow taking the worst of both.

Published by Affirm Press in 2021
28 Thistlethwaite Street, South Melbourne,
Boon Wurrung Country, VIC 3205.
affirmpress.com.au
10 9 8 7 6 5 4 3 2 1

Title: Every Baby Name (Ruined) /
Brian Kerr, author
ISBN: 9781922626202 (hardback)

 A catalogue record for this
book is available from the
National Library of Australia

Cover and internal design by Emily Thiang
Printed in China by C&C Offset Printing Co., Ltd.